THE
GENIUS KID'S
GUIDE TO
CATS

BY MERRIAM GARCIA

North Star
KIDS

TABLE OF CONTENTS

HISTORY OF
DOMESTICATED CATS

Scientists believe that around 8,000 or even 12,000 years ago, wildcats made their ways to farms in what was known as the Fertile Crescent. Today, that area is called the Middle East. These wildcats hunted rodents at the farms. The farmers liked this, so they allowed the cats to stay. This was the start of cats becoming domesticated.

Over time, humans gave the cats food and shelter. The cats changed to fit this environment and became tame.

Eventually, cat populations spread across the world. Cats were very useful on ships, where they hunted mice. And cats in Ancient Egypt were deeply respected. Later, people around the world started keeping cats as pets. In the 1800s, people started developing different cat breeds. Today, there are more than 100 different breeds of domestic cats.

Cats make loveable companions for many people.

Some cats, such as the toyger, have been bred to look like wild tigers.

BREED HISTORY

The Abyssinian is one of the oldest cat breeds. Early Abyssinian lovers did not keep breed records. So, the breed's exact origin is unknown.

Near the end of the 1800s, England was involved in a war in Ethiopia. At the time, Ethiopia was known as Abyssinia. Some people think the first Abyssinian cat came to England not long after the fighting ended.

Cat enthusiasts claimed that this first cat was from Abyssinia. That is how the breed got its name. However, scientists later discovered that the Abyssinian cat most likely came from Asia.

APPEARANCE

Abyssinians are known for their distinctive coats. The fur is short, thick, soft, and silky. It is also richly colored. Much of the coat is ticked. Each ticked hair has two or three bands of black, brown, or blue. The cat's undersides, chest, and legs have no ticking.

An Abyssinian's coat color may be ruddy, red, blue, or fawn. Ruddy coats are orange brown with dark-brown or black ticking. Red coats are a warm red color with chocolate brown bands. Blue coats are beige with slate-blue bands. Fawn coats are pink beige with cocoa-brown ticking.

Abyssinians are medium-sized cats with graceful, muscular bodies. Both males and females can weigh between 8 and 12 pounds (3.5 and 5.4 kg).

BEHAVIOR

These busy cats are always on the move. They will play with a toy for hours. But they can be just as amused with a wadded-up piece of paper.

Abyssinians are athletic and smart. They are curious and good at solving problems. You might find your Abyssinian atop a high perch you thought she could not reach. Then you will know she just applied her intelligence to figure out the way up.

KITTENS

Abyssinians can reproduce by six to nine months of age. Like all cats, a female Abyssinian is pregnant for about 63 to 65 days. The mother can have about three litters each year. On average, she gives birth to four kittens in each litter.

BREED HISTORY

The American bobtail breed appeared in the late 1960s. While traveling in Arizona, John and Brenda Sanders found a short-tailed brown tabby cat. Back home in Iowa, the cat mated with their long-tailed cat. The kittens had short tails. Breeders worked with these bobtail kittens to create the American bobtail.

APPEARANCE

These cats come in many colors. Some American bobtails are the usual colors of black, brown, cream, or white. Others range from red to blue to lavender.

In addition to their wide range of colors, bobtails have a large variety of coat patterns. For example, some have a spotted coat pattern. Others have stripes. Still others have both.

American bobtail cats may have short or long hair. The short-haired bobtail's coat is soft and plush. The long-haired bobtail has medium to long hair, but the coat resists matting.

These cats are big and muscular. Their powerful, athletic bodies are moderately long. With all that muscle, males weigh between 12 and 16 pounds (5.4 and 7.3 kg). Females weigh 7 to 11 pounds (3.2 to 5 kg).

BEHAVIOR

These cats are lively without being overly active. They are clownish and love to play. They'll even learn to play fetch. In fact, some owners say their bobtails are like dogs.

Most American bobtails are highly social. They love the entire family rather than just one person. In addition, this breed gets along with respectful small children and even the family dog.

American bobtail cats are also very smart. Bobtails have the mysterious ability to free themselves from locked cages and rooms. Owners catch them standing on their hind legs, using their front paws to turn doorknobs.

KITTENS

American bobtails mature more slowly than other cat breeds. They take two to three years to fully develop. However, most cats are ready to reproduce by five months of age. Litters of four kittens are most common.

BREED HISTORY

In June 1981, Joe and Grace Ruga discovered a pair of kittens outside their California home. They took the kittens in and named them Shulamith and Panda. Within two weeks, Panda disappeared. But Shulamith, who had curled ears, became a member of the Ruga family.

In December, Shulamith had a litter of kittens. Two of the four kittens had curled ears like their mother. The Rugas realized they may have discovered a new breed of cat. This breed became known as the American curl.

APPEARANCE

American curl cats can have either long or short coats. Both kinds of coats are soft and silky and lie close to the body. The long-haired American curl has a full, plumed tail. The tail of a short-haired curl has the same length of coat as the rest of its body.

The American curl's coat has two layers. The undercoat keeps the cat warm. The outercoat keeps out water. American curl cats have very little undercoat. This breed does not shed as much as some other cats, so it needs less grooming.

Long or short, the coats of American curls come in any color. They also come in many patterns. They can be solid, shaded, smoke, tabby, bicolored, parti-color, or pointed.

BEHAVIOR

American curl cats are playful and curious. They keep a kitten-like personality even as they age. American curl cats make great family pets. They are gentle, affectionate, and faithful. This makes them good with children and other pets. Some say they are like dogs because they will follow their owners around. They don't want to miss anything.

American curls will pat their owners to get attention. This breed is not very talkative. But American curls make cooing sounds when they are curious.

KITTENS

American curl cats are born with straight ears. In three to five days, the ears start to curl backward. But they aren't fully curled until the kitten is 16 weeks old.

BREED HISTORY

The American wirehair cat's story began in 1966, when a litter of kittens was born at Council Rock Farm in Verona, New York. Several had unusual wiry coats. Unfortunately, a weasel attacked the kittens. Only one survived.

Local breeder Joan O'Shea heard about the strange litter. O'Shea visited the farm and bought the surviving kitten. She named the red-and-white tabby male Adam. O'Shea bred Adam, which produced more kittens with wiry coats. One named Amy later gave birth to additional wiry-coated kittens.

Scientists eventually determined that the strange coat was caused by a natural genetic mutation. They also learned that the mutation was incomplete. This meant that not every kitten in a litter would have wiry hair. Some might have only a little. Others may have hair that loses its crimp with age.

APPEARANCE

American wirehair cats have coarse, crimped hair. Even their whiskers and the hair inside their ears is crimped, hooked, or bent. If it is long, the wiry hair can form ringlets. The American wirehair's coat is thick and dense, and it sheds moderately.

There are more than 27 possible color and pattern variations for this breed's coat. Colors include white, blue, cream, red, silver, brown, and tortoiseshell. A tortie's coat is a mix of two colors. The coat's pattern can be solid, bicolored, calico, smoke, chinchilla, or tabby.

Males can grow to weigh more than 12 pounds (5.4 kg). Adult females are slightly smaller. They average 8 to 12 pounds (3.5 to 5.4 kg).

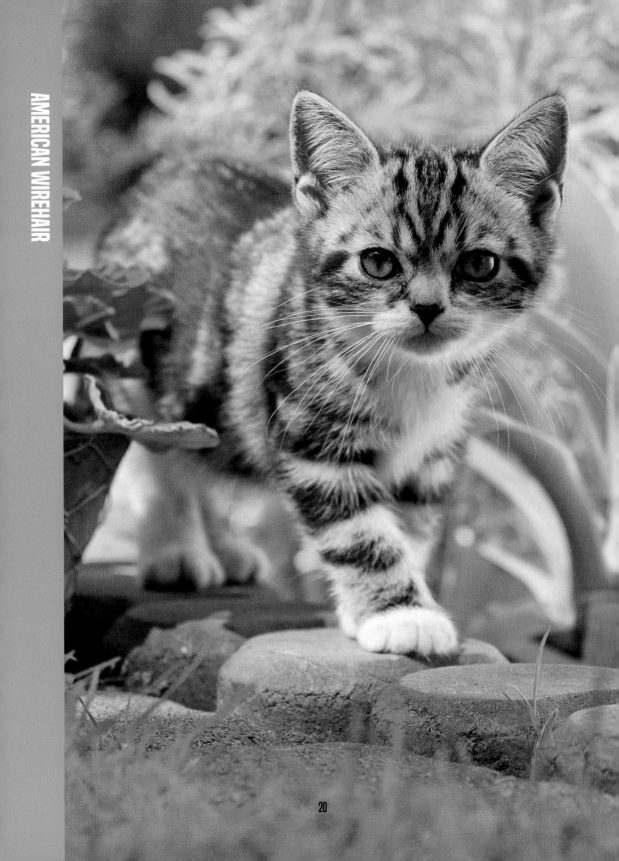

BEHAVIOR

These cats have a soft voice, which they do not use often. They love to play but are not too active. Some owners have described their wirehairs as acting like clowns.

If American wirehairs feel like playing, they may bring a toy to one of their humans as a hint. If they have no toy, they will create one from whatever they can find.

The easygoing wirehair usually gets along with all family members and pets. This makes these cats good additions to the family. However, wirehairs do not need another cat, dog, or human to play with them. So, they also do well in one-owner households.

This breed is a good choice for owners who do not want lap cats. Many wirehairs like to be around their owners but not necessarily on them. They are content with lingering nearby rather than on a lap or couch. Some wirehairs may follow their people from room to room.

KITTENS

Female American wirehair cats can begin having litters around seven to nine months of age. Litters have an average of four to six kittens.

BALINESE

BREED HISTORY

Balinese cats are Siamese cats with long-haired coats. In the 1950s, cats owned by Siamese breeders Marion Dorsey and Helen Smith had long-haired kittens. Dorsey and Smith decided to breed more of these beautiful cats. In 1955, the first long-haired Siamese was entered in a cat show.

People loved the new look. However, breeders wanted the long-haired Siamese to have a different name. The cat's grace reminded Smith of Balinese dancers. So she suggested the name *Balinese*. The name was accepted.

APPEARANCE

The Balinese cat is best known for its soft, silky, long-haired coat. On the body, the coat is 1.5 to 2 inches (4 to 5 cm) long. The fur on the long, plumed tail can be 5 inches (13 cm) long. The Balinese's coat has only one layer. There is no undercoat. This makes the coat lie flat against the cat's body.

The Balinese's coat can be any color. The most common are the traditional Siamese colors of seal, chocolate, blue, and lilac point coats. Females often weigh between 8 to 12 pounds (3.5 to 5.4 kg). Males are slightly larger. They can weigh more than 12 pounds (5.4 kg).

BEHAVIOR

Balinese cats are curious. They love to play. They demand a lot of attention. Balinese also get into a lot of mischief. Do not leave your Balinese cat alone for long periods of time.

Balinese cats make great family pets. They are very loving. They can be good with children and other pets. These cats want to be involved in everything you do.

Like Siamese cats, Balinese are talkative. Sometimes they even talk to themselves. But their voices are softer than a Siamese cat's. If you want a vocal, affectionate, playful cat, the Balinese is the breed for you.

KITTENS

When they reach seven to 12 months old, Balinese cats can reproduce. Usually, four kittens are born in a single litter.

BREED HISTORY

The Bengal cat is a cross between a wildcat called the Asian leopard cat and a domestic house cat. Cat lover Jean Mill founded the Bengal cat. In the early 1960s, Mill bought a female Asian leopard cat. The wildcat mated with a black tomcat and had a female kitten. The kitten grew up and had kittens of her own.

Years later, Mill began working with Dr. Willard Centerwall. Centerwall wanted to address the problem of leukemia in cats. He knew Asian leopard cats did not get the disease as often as house cats. So he crossed several Asian leopard cats with domestic cats. Mill adopted Centerwall's hybrid cats. She wanted to use them to breed domestic cats that looked like wildcats.

In 1980, Mill found a domestic tomcat in India with a leopard-like coat. She took the cat back to the United States. There, she began breeding him with female hybrids. Most modern Bengal cats can be traced back to that tomcat from India.

APPEARANCE

The Bengal cat has been bred to look like a wildcat. Its thick, short fur is either spotted or marbled. Spots with at least two colors or shades in them are called rosettes.

A popular color for the Bengal cat is brown tabby. This cat displays a yellow to orange coat with contrasting dark markings. Three other main colors are seal lynx point tabby, seal sepia tabby, and seal mink tabby. There are also snow leopard, silver, blue, and solid black Bengal cats. Adult Bengal cats can range in size from 8 to 15 pounds (3.5 to 7 kg). They can be 8 to 10 inches (20 to 25 cm) tall.

BEHAVIOR

The behavior of the Bengal cat reflects its wild background. This domestic cat is quick and active. It likes to jump, somersault, and climb. The Bengal cat also loves water. In fact, this hybrid has been known to jump into a running shower.

In addition to its energetic personality, the Bengal cat is highly intelligent. It can be trained to walk on a leash. And it can learn simple tricks such as rolling over.

Many people enjoy the Bengal cat's affectionate, playful nature. However, this hybrid is not a good fit for everyone. People who do not have time for play should not take on a Bengal cat. And some states don't allow Bengal cats because they are part wildcat.

KITTENS

At birth, Bengal kittens are tiny and helpless. Their senses begin working about ten to 12 days after they are born.

BREED HISTORY

Birman cats originated in Burma. There, Birman cats lived in religious temples. They were considered sacred animals.

In 1919, one of these temples was attacked. Two men, Gordon Russell and Auguste Pavie, helped save the temple's priests. The priests were grateful for their help.

Russell and Pavie later moved to France. To thank them, the priests sent the men a pair of Birman cats. The male did not survive the trip. But the female cat arrived safely. And she was pregnant. Her kittens established the Birman breed in the area.

APPEARANCE

The Birman's coat is medium to long. It is thicker around the cat's neck and slightly curly on its stomach. The Birman has many coat colors. Seal point Birmans have fawn to cream bodies and seal-brown points. Blue point Birmans have bluish-white to ivory bodies. Their points are blue. Chocolate point Birmans have ivory bodies and chocolate-brown points. Lilac point cats have a white body. Their points are a light pink-gray color. These cats can weigh between 7 to 12 pounds (3 to 5.4 kg).

BEHAVIOR

Many owners describe their Birmans as social, playful, and entertaining. Other Birmans are reportedly mellow, observant, and loving. They will play for a while and then retreat to a quiet spot.

However, this spot out of the action will still be in the company of others. Birman cats love companionship. They make wonderful pets for people who spend much of their time at home. Those who are often away from home should consider a pet companion for their Birman.

KITTENS

Birman cats are ready to reproduce at five to six months of age. Mother Birmans usually give birth to four kittens in a litter. Birman kittens should be handled every day. Daily contact will create calm, friendly pets.

BREED HISTORY

Nikki Horner of Kentucky created Bombays in 1958. She wanted miniature black panthers with copper eyes. So Horner crossed a black American shorthair and a sable Burmese to create this breed. Bombay cats resemble the black leopard of India. So they were named after the city of Bombay, India.

APPEARANCE

Bombay cats have a shiny, jet-black coat. It is short, close lying, and satiny. Bombays are medium-sized cats. Their bodies are strong, firm, and muscular. They can weigh between 6 and 11 pounds (3 and 5 kg).

BEHAVIOR

Bombays are ideal family pets. They are affectionate cats who love attention and do not like to be left alone. If Bombays are going to be left alone, they prefer another cat to play with.

Bombay cats are fairly quiet. They have a soft but distinctive voice. They are playful cats without being hyperactive. Bombay cats are intelligent, confident, and friendly.

KITTENS

Bombays have about four kittens per litter. These kittens can have brown, blue, or green eyes when they are born. Then, their eyes turn to a gold or copper color when they're around a year old.

BREED HISTORY

The British shorthair cat's permanent smile has made this very old breed famous. The well-known breed traces its history back to ancient Rome. The Romans brought their cats with them to Britain. There, the cats became important mouse catchers.

In the late 1800s, humans began refining the breed based on color and other qualities. In 1871, British shorthair cats, or Brits, appeared in the first formal cat show held in England.

APPEARANCE

The British shorthair has a short, dense coat. Brits can be a variety of solid colors. They are most known for blue. Brits can also be white, black, red, cream, chocolate, or lavender. Some have tabby or tortoiseshell coats.

This charming breed also has a wide range of eye colors. Copper, gold, hazel, green, blue green, and sapphire blue are all possible. Sometimes, a Brit's eyes are each a different color.

The Brit is one of the larger cat breeds. A full-grown male weighs about 9 to 17 pounds (4 to 8 kg). A female is slightly smaller, weighing 7 to 12 pounds (3 to 5.4 kg).

BEHAVIOR

British shorthair cats are great house cats for families on the go. They are easygoing, nondestructive, low-energy pets. They do not need other animals for company. But they have a good temperament for getting along with children, dogs, birds, and other cats.

Brits have a calm, quiet nature. They will curl up next to you on the couch to be petted. But they are not the type of cat to curl up on a lap. They typically do not like to be picked up and held.

Brits are patient, intelligent animals, so animal trainers enjoy working with them. These cats also like playing with toys. They can even learn to play fetch.

KITTENS

As mothers, British shorthairs are loving and attentive. They can have up to three litters per year. Each litter usually contains four to five large kittens.

BREED HISTORY

In 1930, an American doctor named Joseph Thompson imported a cat from Burma to the United States. The cat's name was Wong Mau. Thompson believed Wong Mau was a new breed.

Thompson wanted to develop the breed. He thought the Siamese breed was the closest in looks and temperament to Wong Mau. So, he mated Wong Mau with a Siamese cat. Wong Mau's kittens were the first Burmese cats.

In 1949, Lilian France imported some of Wong Mau's kittens to England. She bred the kittens with Siamese cats. Over time, the Burmese cats in England and the United States became two separate breeds. Today, the cats from the United States are known as Burmese. The English cats are known as European Burmese.

APPEARANCE

The Burmese has a short coat with almost no undercoat. The coat is dense and lies close to the body. The fur is shiny, fine, and satiny. Its main colors are sable, champagne, blue, and platinum. Sable is the most common shade.

Burmese are medium-sized cats with a rounded body. They are often much heavier than they appear. The average Burmese weighs about 8 pounds (4 kg). The males are usually a bit larger than the females.

The European Burmese also has a short coat. It can be a variety of solid colors. The most common colors are brown, blue, chocolate, lilac, red, and cream. The coat is often lighter in color on the cat's belly than it is on its back. European Burmese also come in tortoiseshell.

The European Burmese is a medium-sized cat. These cats can weigh between 7 to 14 pounds (3 to 6 kg), with the females being smaller than the males.

Burmese

BEHAVIOR

Both Burmese and European Burmese cats are playful. They love attention. They follow their owners around and sit on people's laps. These two breeds desire company. They do not like to be left alone for long periods of time.

Burmese and European Burmese cats are intelligent. They can be taught to do tricks, such as fetching. They can also learn commands such as "sit."

One difference between the European Burmese (*pictured*) and the Burmese is their eyes. Burmese have rounder eyes, while European Burmese have a top line that slants inward.

KITTENS

Burmese have about five kittens in each litter. European Burmese have around four kittens at a time. When Burmese and European Burmese kittens are between 12 and 16 weeks old, they are old enough to leave their mothers. They can be adopted by a loving family.

BURMILLA

BREED HISTORY

The Burmilla first appeared in England in 1981. That year, a Burmese cat named Bambino Lilac Fabergé (fah-behr-zhay) escaped from her home. She mated with a chinchilla Persian cat named Jemari Sanquist. Their kittens were the first Burmillas.

APPEARANCE

Burmillas can have long or short coats. Those with short coats have soft, fine, silky fur. The fur lays close to the body. Longhair Burmillas have the same fine, silky fur, but it is longer. They also have fluffy tails and tufts on their ears.

Burmillas are known for the color of their coats. They have silver undercoats. The fur of the topcoat can be tipped or shaded. Tipped coats have color on the tip of each hair. Shaded coats have color on one-third of each hair. This type of coloring gives the Burmilla a silvery, shimmering appearance. The coat can be shaded or tipped in 13 colors. These include brown, blue, red, chocolate, lilac, and tortoiseshell.

Burmillas are medium-sized cats. When they are fully grown, they weigh between 8 and 12 pounds (3.5 and 5.4 kg).

BEHAVIOR

Burmillas are known for their sweet dispositions. These cats are gentle, playful, and curious. They love spending time with their owners. Burmillas make good pets for families with young children and other animals.

The personality of a Burmilla is a mix of traits from its Persian and Burmese relatives. Burmillas are outgoing and friendly, just like the Burmese. Like Persians, Burmillas are relaxed and calm.

Burmillas love to have fun. They often act like kittens even when they are adults. They enjoy playing with their owners and their toys. Burmillas are also smart cats. Some have been known to use their paws to open cupboard doors and turn on faucets.

KITTENS

When a female cat delivers her litter, it is called kittening. A Burmilla will have about six kittens in a litter.

CALICO COLOR HISTORY

Calico is the term people use to describe a certain color pattern in a cat's coat. Calico cats most likely originated in Asia. There, these cats were considered lucky charms. They were revered for the rarity of their curious coloring.

Male calicoes are even more unusual. This is because most calicoes are female. The gene that causes the calico's distinct coloring is sex-linked. Only about one in 3,000 calico cats is male. And a male calico usually can't produce offspring.

APPEARANCE

All calico cats have a tricolored coat. Most are white with splotches of orange and black. Some calicoes have coats of white, cream, and gray. These are called dilute calicoes. The calico's coat can be long or short, depending on the breed.

Calicoes come in various sizes, depending on the breed. Most weigh between 6 and 10 pounds (3 and 5 kg). Some cats can weigh as much as 28 pounds (13 kg). Female cats are usually smaller than males.

BEHAVIOR

Besides its coloring, there are not many qualities specific to the calico. Its personality often depends on the breed.

Most cats are very independent. But if properly cared for and socialized, your calico should be friendly and affectionate. Cats usually have calm, charming natures. And most cats enjoy companions, such as other cats, dogs, or children.

KITTENS

Calico kittens pop up in litters of many different breeds. It's impossible to plan a litter consisting completely of calicoes. Getting the correct coat coloring is like a game of chance.

BREED HISTORY

The Chartreux is one of the oldest domestic cat breeds. Many historians believe the breed originated in what is now Syria. Legends tell of Crusaders bringing the cats back to French monasteries.

The Crusaders left the cats with Carthusian monks, which is where some people think their name comes from. These prized mousers protected important papers from gnawing rodents. And they killed snakes. Others believe the Chartreux got its name from a fine Spanish wool. Animals were often named for their features. In this case, the breed's dense, woolly coat closely resembled the wool.

APPEARANCE

The Chartreux has a special and beautiful coat. In the cat world, its color is called blue. The Chartreux's coat comes in shades of gray from slate to ash. The ends of the hairs have a hint of silver. The Chartreux's coat has two layers. The dense undercoat has a soft, plush feel. It helps keep the animal warm. The medium-short outercoat keeps out water. On average, males weigh 10 to 14 pounds (4.5 to 6.4 kg). Females are more often between 6 and 9 pounds (2.7 and 4 kg).

BEHAVIOR

Chartreux are loving and calm. This easygoing character makes them good with children. They make nice family pets, but they will attach themselves to one person. These loyal cats will follow their favorite person constantly.

Chartreux enjoy fetching, chasing, and other play. They are also very intelligent. Some respond to their names. And they enjoy learning tricks. Chartreux have been known to open latches and push buttons.

Chartreux are quieter than some breeds. They make their needs known with soft meows. When highly interested or entertained, Chartreux chirp. They also have expressive faces, ears, and tails.

KITTENS

Like all domestic cats, Chartreux newborn kittens are nearly helpless. After ten to 12 days, they can see and hear. Around this time, each kitten's first teeth have come in. At first, kittens drink their mother's milk. By six to seven weeks, Chartreux kittens are eating just solid foods.

BREED HISTORY

People were breeding chausie cats in the late 1960s and early 1970s. At that time, many people liked the idea of having a jungle cat for a pet. However, jungle cats are wild animals. They don't make good pets.

Some breeders thought mixing jungle cats with house cats might be the answer. They hoped to create a cat that looked like a jungle cat. But they wanted it to have the personality of a domestic cat. Early breeders crossed many different house cats with jungle cats to create chausies. Breeders eventually settled on two domestic cats, the Abyssinian and the domestic shorthair. Today, some states don't allow people to own cats such as chausies.

APPEARANCE

Chausie coats feature short- to medium-length fur. The fur is dense and a bit coarse. Chausie breeders recognize three colors of chausie cats. These are solid black, brown ticked tabby, and black grizzled ticked tabby. All of these colors are found in jungle cats. Chausies weigh between 15 and 30 pounds (7 and 14 kg). They stand 14 to 18 inches (36 to 46 cm) tall at the shoulders.

BEHAVIOR

Chausie owners say their pets are good-natured, loyal, and affectionate. In fact, some owners say their chausies are a lot like dogs. These owners have trained their chausies to walk on a leash and play fetch.

Like their wild ancestors, chausies are very active. They sleep less than other house cats. And they are more active in the evening.

Chausies are smart animals. They can easily become bored, which can lead to trouble. An owner should give a chausie plenty of attention and toys. The owner may even need to consider getting another cat for the chausie to play with.

KITTENS

Most smaller female cats give birth to kittens about two months after mating. Kittens are born completely helpless.

Most owners train their chausies to use a litter box. This can be a challenge, however. Some chausies may not be very far removed from their wild jungle cat relatives. Those chausies may not want to use a litter box.

CORNISH REX

BREED HISTORY

Cornish rex cats are easily recognized by their curly, plush coats. For this reason, they are sometimes called the poodle cat.

Cornish rexes were first bred in Cornwall, England. In 1950, Nina Ennismore's farm cat had a litter of kittens. One of the kittens had curly hair. Ennismore bred the curly-haired kitten with its mother and the Cornish rex breed was developed.

APPEARANCE

Most cats have coats that are made up of three different layers of hair. But Cornish rexes only have one layer: a soft undercoat. This gives Cornish rexes their distinctive look.

Cornish rexes come in many different colors. They can be white, black, blue, red, smoke, tabby, or tortoiseshell. Most Cornish rexes have gold or green eyes, except for the pointed rex, which has blue eyes. The color of a Cornish rex's nose and paw pads corresponds with its coat color.

The Cornish rex is a small to medium-sized cat. Males can weigh around 8 to 10 pounds (3.6 to 4.5 kg). Females weigh around 5 to 7 pounds (2.3 to 3 kg).

BEHAVIOR

Cornish rex cats are ideal family pets. They are playful, friendly, and good with children. They are energetic and can be quite vocal at times.

Cornish rexes quickly become attached to their owners, and they love to be around people. So Cornish rex cats do not do well when left alone for long periods of time. If you are gone all day, consider getting two of them so they have company.

Some Cornish rexes will walk on a leash, greet you at the door, and even fetch a small ball. These lovable cats are social, intelligent, and curious.

KITTENS

Cornish rexes have three or four kittens per litter.

DEVON REX

BREED HISTORY

In 1959, a stray tomcat with a curly coat lived in Buckfastleigh in Devon, England. So did Beryl Cox. One day, Cox adopted a stray female cat with a normal, straight tortie-and-white coat. Her new pet soon had a litter of kittens. A male from the litter was born with a curly coat and pointy ears like the tomcat. Cox liked the kitten's special look, funny personality, and loving nature. She named him Kirlee.

Cox knew the Cornish rex breed had been discovered ten years before. She felt Kirlee could add to this breed. So, she sold him to a breeder in 1960. But Kirlee had a different type of rex gene. Breeders called it *Gene II*. Kirlee couldn't be a Cornish rex. He began an entirely new breed of cat, the Devon rex.

APPEARANCE

The Devon rex's name reveals something special about its coat. The coat is rexed. Cats with this type of coat have very short guard hairs or none at all. Guard hairs are the long, coarse hairs that protect a cat's undercoat. The Devon rex breed has guard hairs, but there are fewer of them. They also vary in length. This is what gives the coat a lumpy or wavy feeling. A Devon rex weighs 6 to 9 pounds (3 to 4 kg). Males are heavier than females.

BEHAVIOR

These cats quickly learn tricks and will play tag, fetch, and hide-and-seek. They want to be involved in everything. Devon rex cats will wag their tails like dogs and follow their humans everywhere. They are people pleasers, even coming when their names are called. Devon rex cats get along well with other pets and children. That's important, because this breed does not like being left alone.

KITTENS

A Devon rex kitten may not yet have the coat you would expect. Devon rex cats are born with fur. But at eight weeks old, they molt. They will be left with a downy coat on their stomachs that is soft like suede. It can take anywhere from a few days to a year for a new coat to grow. The new coat will have the wavy look of the rexes.

BREED HISTORY

In ancient Egypt, cats were treated with much respect. One exotic-looking cat breed that came from ancient Egypt is the Egyptian mau. It is believed that the spotted cats painted on ancient Egyptian walls are the early ancestors of this breed. This would make the Egyptian mau one of the oldest known breeds.

APPEARANCE

A mau's spots and stripes give it the appearance of an exotic African wildcat. Its spots range in size and shape. The legs and tail are striped. The cat has marks on its cheeks called mascara lines. The mau also wears an *M* marking on its forehead. Maus can have different coat colors, such as silver, smoke, or bronze. They can weigh between 6 to 14 pounds (3 to 6 kg).

BEHAVIOR

To interact with their human companions, maus will often chortle or chirp like birds. A wiggle of the tail shows they are happy.

This social breed enjoys attention and being fussed over. It takes great pleasure in cuddling, which can make the mau ideal for families. Maus are curious, playful cats. They love to investigate their surroundings.

KITTENS

Most female cats can have kittens by 12 months of age. Mother maus are pregnant for about 67 days. The average litter size is three to six kittens.

BREED HISTORY

Exotic shorthair cats are Persian cats with shorter fur. Legends say Persian cats came from Persia in the 1600s. This area became modern-day Iran.

In the late 1950s, several US breeders crossed short-haired cats with Persians. The kittens had a Persian cat's features but not the Persian's long coat. The kittens had round faces, stocky frames, and plush, short coats. The breed was eventually named the exotic shorthair. The cats seemed exotic because the breed had a different look than other cats.

APPEARANCE

The exotic shorthair's coat isn't like the coat of any other short-haired cat. The cat's medium-length fur is an even length on the body. It is shorter on the cat's face and legs. The coat is also very dense. No other breed has a coat like it.

The exotic shorthair's coat can be any color. The most common are blue, black, cream, red, tortoiseshell, and tabby. These cats can weigh up to 15 pounds (6.8 kg).

BEHAVIOR

Exotic shorthair cats are gentle and calm. They do not demand a lot of attention, but they love to be near people. These cats are playful. But they are also independent enough to be left alone.

KITTENS

Most cats are able to mate when they are seven to 12 months old. However, exotic shorthair cats mature slower than other cats. They may not be ready to reproduce until they are older. There are usually four kittens per litter.

BREED HISTORY

Hundreds of years ago, naturally all-brown cats existed in Siam, which is now Thailand. In the late 1800s, travelers brought these brown cats to Great Britain. These unusual cats were popular for a while. But in the 1920s, they disappeared from cat shows.

In the 1950s, some English breeders wanted to bring back green-eyed, solid brown cats. So they bred domestic shorthair cats, Siamese cats, and Russian blue cats to create the Havana brown cat.

APPEARANCE

The Havana brown's coat features short- to medium-length fur. These cats are known for their rich, glossy coats. They are solid chocolate brown, reddish-brown, or mahogany in color. Havana browns are also known for their vivid green eyes.

Adults weigh an average of 6 to 10 pounds (2.5 to 4.5 kg). Females are slightly smaller than males.

BEHAVIOR

Havana browns are unique in how they learn about their surroundings. Most cats rely on their sense of smell. But graceful Havana brown cats also use their paws. They are more likely than other breeds to explore things by touching and feeling them.

This breed is intelligent and affectionate. They crave attention and will often reach out and touch their humans or raise a paw in greeting. They are happy to cuddle up with their owners or with other cats. In fact, they are happiest when they can be involved in everything their owners do.

Havana browns speak in quiet, gentle voices. With enough attention, Havana brown cats do very well in single-owner homes. These playful pets can also get along with other pets, including dogs.

KITTENS

Mother Havana browns usually have litters of two to four kittens. Often, Havana brown kittens have light tabby markings. These fade over time. The coat usually turns into its signature reddish-brown color within two years. Other kittens are born with lilac-colored fur and whiskers.

HIMALAYAN

BREED HISTORY

The Himalayan cat breed began as an experiment in genetics. In the 1930s, scientists bred Siamese and Persian cats together. They wanted to see if the Siamese's color pattern could be passed to the long-haired Persian.

From this experiment, the first pointed longhair cat was born. This cat was recognized as the beginning of the Himalayan breed. Throughout the 1950s, programs worked to establish a Persian-type breed with Siamese markings.

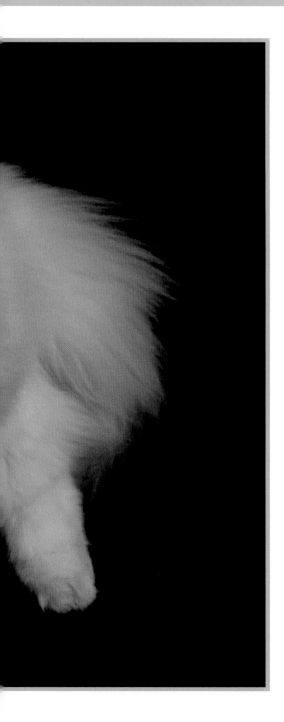

These programs officially introduced the Himalayan into the cat family.

APPEARANCE

The Himalayan has the long, thick coat of a Persian. But it has the distinct color pattern of a Siamese. The Himalayan carries the pointing gene that causes this coloration. The pointing gene uses body temperature to determine color. The ears, face, tail, and legs are usually colder than the rest of the body. So, the fur in these areas is darker. But in warmer areas, the gene prevents the darker color from developing. Most Himalayans have bright blue eyes. Some have gold eyes. These cats can weigh 11 to 13 pounds (5 to 6 kg).

BEHAVIOR

Like their Persian cousins, Himalayans are sweet tempered and calm. Like Siamese, they are outgoing and playful. Himalayans adore attention.

These cats make perfect indoor pets. They don't like jumping or climbing and are not very adventurous. They like to follow their families around and snuggle in laps.

KITTENS

Female Himalayan cats give birth to approximately four kittens in each litter. Kittens are born completely white with pink noses. Faint point markings start filling in during the first week. The pattern might take up to 18 months to develop.

JAPANESE BOBTAIL

BREED HISTORY

Japanese bobtail cats are best known for their short pom-pom tails. No one knows how they came to have these unique tails. But Japan is an island nation. The island kept the cats isolated, which allowed the mutation to develop in the population.

APPEARANCE

Most Japanese bobtail cats have soft, medium-length coats. However, some Japanese bobtails are long-haired. Short or long, Japanese bobtail coats come in many different colors and patterns.

Tabby bobtails are white with brown, red, blue, cream, or silver striping. Japanese bobtails can also have calico fur. Or the fur can be solid black, blue, red, cream, or white.

Most people identify the Japanese bobtail by its unique tail. The tail actually grows to about 4 to 5 inches (10 to 12.7 cm) long. However, it is kinked or curved to about 3 inches (7.6 cm) from the cat's body. These cats weigh from 6 to 10 pounds (2.5 to 4.5 kg) when fully mature. Females are slightly smaller than males.

BEHAVIOR

The Japanese bobtail cat is ideal for people seeking an active, affectionate family member. It has a loving, outgoing personality. This high-energy breed loves to play and is especially good with children. Bobtails are at their best with constant companionship.

These bright felines like to keep busy hiding and exploring. Inquisitive and alert, these cats also remain masters of the pounce, so they are skilled hunters.

KITTENS

Japanese bobtail females usually have three or four kittens in a litter. Japanese bobtail kittens are usually more active at an earlier age than other breeds of kittens.

KORAT

BREED HISTORY

For hundreds of years, Korat cats have been prized in Thailand. Korats are named for the province of Korat, Thailand. There they are seen as symbols of success.

In 1959, the Korat breed came to the United States. Today, Korats are rare all over the world, even in their native Thailand.

APPEARANCE

Korats have short, glossy coats. The coat lies close to the skin because it does not have an undercoat. The fine hair feels satiny to the touch. Korat cats are silver-blue all over. The tips of their hairs have a silvery sheen. Korat cats can weigh 5 to 11 pounds (2 to 5 kg).

BEHAVIOR

Korats have strong personalities. They are affectionate with their owners. But these cats don't always like strangers. Sometimes Korats even hiss at them.

Intelligence is one quality of Korat cats. They can be taught to walk on a leash and do tricks. These cats are also very playful and active. But if not given the proper attention, Korats can be demanding and stubborn.

KITTENS

A Korat usually has a litter of four or five kittens. Bright green eyes are one feature of Korats. Kittens may have blue eyes that turn to amber, and then to green.

KURILIAN BOBTAIL

BREED HISTORY

Kurilian bobtails come from the Kuril Islands, a chain of islands between Russia and Japan. The cats have lived there for more than 200 years. No one is certain how the cats came to live on the islands. Some people believe they arrived on fishing boats. These boats often had cats on board to control rodents. Some of the cats may have escaped when the boats docked there.

APPEARANCE

A Kurilian bobtail's coat can be either short or semi-long. In both cases, the coat is fine and dense. The fur feels soft and silky. It lies flat against the cat's body.

Kurilian bobtails can come in a variety of colors. The breed does not have one specific color or pattern. They can be cream, black, red, orange, or silver. The patterns on Kurilian bobtails also show great variety. Some of the cats in this breed are one solid color. The tabby pattern has stripes and spots. The tortoiseshell pattern is a mix of two colors, usually orange and black.

Adult males can weigh up to 15 pounds (7 kg). Adult females weigh between 8 and 11 pounds (4 and 5 kg).

BEHAVIOR

Kurilian bobtails are playful, social animals. These loyal cats love to be around their owners. Kurilian bobtails are gentle, calm, and friendly. They make great pets for families with children, dogs, and other cats.

At home, Kurilians love to seek out the highest point they can find. They climb on top of bookcases, cabinets, and doorways. This is part of their hunting instincts. It allows them to observe a large area from one place.

Kurilian bobtails are smart. Often, they only need to be shown something once before they understand what they are supposed to do. Kurilians are also a quiet breed. They make soft noises that sound like a bird chirping.

KITTENS

The female Kurilian bobtail usually has three to five kittens in a litter.

MAINE COON

BREED HISTORY

The Maine coon cat is native to the state of Maine. Early settlers brought short-haired cats to the area. Later, long-haired cats arrived on merchant ships from Europe. The two cat types mated, and their descendants became Maine coon cats.

APPEARANCE

Maine coon cats have long, shaggy coats. The breed developed this thick coat for protection against harsh New England winters. The coat protects the cat from rain, snow, and cold.

Maine coon cat coats come in many different colors, such as white, black, blue, red, and cream. They can also be tabby, tabby and white, bicolored, and parti-color. There are three coat patterns. They are classic, mackerel, and patched.

Most Maine coon cats have brown tabby coats. Their eyes can be shades of green, gold, or copper. White Maine coon cats may have blue eyes, or each eye might be a different color.

The Maine coon cat is a large cat with a muscular body. It can weigh between 12 to 18 pounds (5.4 to 8 kg). Females are smaller than males.

BEHAVIOR

Maine coon cats are sturdy, gentle, and loyal animals. They are also sweet, loving pets. In fact, they get along well with kids and dogs.

These easygoing, affectionate cats like to be around their people. But Maine coon cats are not lap cats. While they love to socialize, they remain independent.

Maine coon cats love to play, even when they are older. These big cats are also very vocal. They communicate with high-pitched chirps and mews.

KITTENS

A Maine coon cat can reproduce when it is seven to 12 months old. A female may have three litters each year. Each litter will have about four kittens. These kittens grow slowly and don't reach full size until around age three.

BREED HISTORY

The Manx cat got its start hundreds of years ago on the Isle of Man. This island nation lies in the Irish Sea. It sits between the islands of Great Britain and Ireland.

As the Isle of Man is an island, many ships docked there. Cats that arrived on the ships went ashore. There, they mated with local domestic cats. At some point in time, a mutation occurred in the cats. This change caused kittens to be born without tails.

The tailless cats became common on the Isle of Man. These unusual cats charmed travelers. Visitors began to take the cats back to their home countries.

APPEARANCE

The Manx cat can have a short or long coat. Both are double coats. The short coat has an outer layer of longer, glossy hairs. These cover a short, cottony undercoat.

Manx cats can be any color or pattern. There are solid, smoke, tabby, and bicolored Manx. The Manx cat's eye color depends on the color of its coat. It can have copper, green, hazel, or blue eyes. Sometimes, each eye is a different color.

Many Manx cats have no tail. There is a slight dimple where the tail should be. These Manx are called rumpies. Manx that have a little cartilage but still no tail are called risers. Those with short tails are called stumpies. Manx with regular tails are called longies. Manx cats can range from 8 to 12 pounds (3.5 to 5.4 kg).

BEHAVIOR

Manx cats are affectionate and loyal. They make sweet, loving pets. These even-tempered cats get along well with kids and dogs. However, Manx also enjoy quiet, relaxed surroundings.

Many people call the Manx the "dog cat." These cats have many dog-like qualities. They can be taught to fetch toys and will sometimes even bury them. The cats can also be protective of their homes.

Manx cats are generally quiet cats. When they do speak up, they have soft voices. But they will not hesitate to give an opinion when necessary.

KITTENS

Manx cats can reproduce once they are seven to 12 months old. Females may have three litters each year. There will be about three to five kittens in each litter. A single litter can include rumpies, risers, stumpies, and longies.

This breed is healthy overall. But some kittens are born with Manx Syndrome. This is a flaw in the kitten's spine.

BREED HISTORY

Many people believe the ancestors of Norwegian forest cats served as mousers on Viking ships. For many centuries, these long-haired cats lived wild in Norway's forests. They later became prized for their hunting skills on Norwegian farms.

APPEARANCE

Norwegian forest cats change coats with the seasons. In winter, a double coat keeps the cat warm and dry. The downy undercoat provides warmth. The long overcoat with its silky, flowing guard hairs protects against water.

In spring, Norwegian forest cats shed their winter undercoats. Their warm-weather coats are shorter and sleeker. Only their tail plumes and toe and ear tufts remain all year.

Norwegian forest cats can come in every possible coat pattern or color combination. The most common are black-and-white or tabby patterned. They can have green or gold eyes. Males weigh 12 to 16 pounds (5.4 to 7 kg). Females are usually lighter, weighing 9 to 12 pounds (4 to 5.4 kg).

BEHAVIOR

The Norwegian forest cat is active and independent. This freedom-loving animal spent much of its history living in forests or on farms. So as a pet, it should not be confined completely indoors.

Norwegian forest cats are often reserved with strangers. But once they get used to a new person, they enjoy company. Sometimes, they select one person to be a special friend. They also enjoy being with other cats, dogs, and children.

KITTENS

A typical litter has about four kittens. Norwegian forest cats change before your eyes. Kittens boast long, woolly coats. But by three months, kittens appear short-haired. Only their bushy tails hint at what's ahead. Sometimes, it takes two years for their coats to develop shaggy ruffs.

BREED HISTORY

The ocicat was developed accidentally in 1964. A breeder from Michigan named Virginia Daly was trying to create an Abyssinian-pointed Siamese cat. She bred a Siamese with an Abyssinian. The litter contained a male kitten with gold spots. This was the beginning of the ocicat breed.

APPEARANCE

Ocicats have short, glossy coats. The coats lie close to ocicats' bodies and have a satiny texture. Their fur is ticked except for on the tip of the tail, which is a solid color. Ocicats have distinctive colored spots.

Ocicats' coats can have different spotted colors. These colors are blue, chocolate, cinnamon, fawn, lavender, and tawny. These cats can also have coats of colored spots on a silver-white background. Ocicats are fairly large, and weigh from 6 to 15 pounds (2.7 to 7 kg).

BEHAVIOR

Despite their wild looks, ocicats are gentle, friendly cats. They get along well with children and other pets. They are loving, playful, and intelligent. Ocicats have many dog-like qualities. They are easy to train. They can be taught to walk on a leash. They will obey voice commands and play fetch.

Ocicats are very active cats. They need plenty of room to run around. They do not like to be left alone for long periods of time.

KITTENS

Ocicats usually have about five kittens per litter. All kittens are born blind and helpless. They need to drink their mothers' milk for the first three weeks. Then they start to eat solid food. Most kittens stop drinking their mothers' milk when they are about eight weeks old.

BREED HISTORY

Oriental shorthair cats are related to Siamese cats. Siamese cats are known for their light-colored coats and dark-colored points. They were introduced to the United States in 1878.

In the late 1950s, Europeans bred solid-colored cats with Siamese cats. These new kittens were many different colors and patterns. At first, each new color and pattern became a new breed. Soon, there were too many colors to have separate breeds. So, all short-haired, non-pointed cats were called Oriental shorthairs.

APPEARANCE

The Oriental shorthair's coat is glossy and lies close to the body. It is satin-like and short all over. This breed's coat can be any color. Solid white, cream, red, ebony, blue, chestnut, lavender, cinnamon, or fawn are common. These nine colors can be combined to create many patterns. An Oriental's coat can be shaded, smoke, parti-color, bicolored, or pointed. Some Oriental coats have the tabby pattern. Members of this breed weigh 9 to 14 pounds (4 to 6 kg). Females are smaller than males.

BEHAVIOR

Oriental shorthair cats are loving and vocal. They want to be near people. If given the attention they need, they will do anything to please their owners. They are unhappy if they are ignored.

Orientals like children, dogs, and other cats. These cats are very playful. They can also entertain themselves with simple toys, such as cardboard boxes.

Oriental shorthairs are very curious and intelligent. They will open drawers, jump on shelves, or dig in bags to find hidden objects.

KITTENS

An Oriental's colors may take some time to develop. Tabby colors can appear right away. Others may not appear until the kitten is one year old.

PERSIAN

BREED HISTORY

The Persian cat's exact beginnings are lost to history. Cat enthusiasts believe the Persian's ancestors are Angora cats from Turkey and long-haired cats from Persia, which is now Iran. These cats arrived in Europe in the 1600s. In 1871, the first British cat show was held in London, England. Persian cats were among the 160 competitors.

APPEARANCE

The Persian cat has a long, thick, flowing coat. This double coat has an outer layer of longer hairs that guard a cottony undercoat. Persians come in many colors. They can be solid, silver or golden, and shaded or smoke. Other Persian colors are tabby, parti-color, calico or bicolored, and Himalayan. The Persian cat's eye color depends on its coat color. It can have blue, orange, gold, green, or copper eyes. Some Persian cats have eyes of two different colors. Males can weigh more than 12 pounds (5.4 kg). Females range from 8 to 12 pounds (4 to 5.4 kg).

BEHAVIOR

Persians are gentle tempered and calm. They make sweet, loving pets. These affectionate cats enjoy a peaceful, secure home. Once they feel safe, they will be happy around children and other pets.

Persians don't like jumping or climbing. Some would even call these cats lazy. But Persians like to play and are very responsive to their owners.

KITTENS

Female Persians give birth to about four kittens in each litter. Persian kittens should be gently cuddled every day. This will create calm, friendly pets. Early handling also prepares them for the daily grooming they need throughout their lives. If they become used to grooming at a young age, they likely won't fight grooming as much when they are older.

BREED HISTORY

In 1985, cat lover Carol Ann Brewer purchased a male kitten that had more toes than normal. He did not just look unusual. His behavior was also different from most house cats.

The kitten's mother was a barn cat. The mother's owner didn't know for sure who the father was. But she claimed he was a bobcat. However, scientists have proved pixiebobs have no bobcat blood. If any breeding between barn cats and bobcats occurred, it happened many years ago.

Because her kitten's background was unclear, Brewer called her new cat a legend cat. Brewer lived in Washington State.

Other people in the area claimed their cats also had wild roots. Brewer took home two more of these legend cats. Two of her three legend cats then mated and had three kittens. Brewer kept the only female kitten and named her Pixie.

Pixie was unlike other cats Brewer had owned. She had a wild-looking face and spotted reddish fawn fur. Pixie inspired Brewer to breed more cats like her. Brewer named her new hybrid after this special kitten.

APPEARANCE

The pixiebob has a thick double coat of fur that stands up off its body. The fur is woolly and can be either long or short. The coat is slightly softer on a long-haired pixiebob than on a short-haired pixiebob. Pixiebobs come in all shades of brown spotted tabby. The spots can be large or small. This hybrid's short tail may be kinked but should still be flexible. The pixiebob has large, thick toes. About 50 percent of these domestic cats have extra toes. Pixiebobs can range from 8 to 17 pounds (4 to 8 kg). The pixiebob has a bobbed tail. It adds just 4 to 6 inches (10 to 15 cm) to this domestic cat's length.

BEHAVIOR

Pixiebobs are active cats that love to play. Without someone to play with, they can become sad. These intelligent cats can fetch. They can also be taught to walk on a leash.

Pixiebobs do best with owners who truly love cats. These domestic cats become very close to their human family members. They get along well with children and other animals. Most pixiebobs rarely meow, and some never do at all. Instead, they communicate with chirps and chitters.

KITTENS

Today, breeders keep this breed true by breeding one pixiebob with another pixiebob. Pixiebobs are large house cats. It takes about four years for kittens to reach full size.

RAGAMUFFIN

BREED HISTORY

In the 1960s, a California cat breeder named Ann Baker took an interest in a litter of kittens from a cat named Josephine. Her kittens were unusually sweet, calm, and friendly. Baker purchased some of the kittens and began to breed them.

From Josephine's kittens, Baker created many breeds. They were called ragdolls, miracle ragdolls, honey bears, doll babies, shu schoos, and catenoids. Baker referred to all of these cats as cherubim (CHEHR–uh–bihm). This means "angels."

Breeders and cat owners alike enjoyed the cherubim breeds and wanted more. But Baker had strict rules about breeding. And she would not let cherubim be recognized by cat groups.

Breeders disliked these harsh rules. In 1993, they formed their own group. They mixed the cherubim breeds together to create RagaMuffins.

APPEARANCE

A cuddly RagaMuffin's coat can be medium or long. The fur is soft and silky. A RagaMuffin's coat comes in a variety of colors. It can be white, black, blue, red, cream, chocolate, lilac, cinnamon, or fawn. Some RagaMuffins are a solid color. Others have patterns such as stripes, spots, or patches that mix several colors. Adult males weigh between 14 and 20 pounds (6 and 9 kg). Adult females weigh 8 to 13 pounds (4 to 6 kg).

BEHAVIOR

RagaMuffins are often compared to teddy bears. They are soft, furry, and love to cuddle. Sometimes, RagaMuffins go limp like a ragdoll when they are being cuddled. It is a sign that they are happy.

Unlike many other cat breeds, RagaMuffins like to be handled. This makes them good pets in homes with children. The easygoing RagaMuffin gets along well with other pets. Like a dog, it greets people at the door.

KITTENS

When a female RagaMuffin is about one year old, she can begin to mate. A RagaMuffin mother will have about five kittens in her litter.

BREED HISTORY

Ragdoll cats did not develop on their own in nature. Rather, a person created the ragdoll breed. That person was cat breeder Ann Baker. Baker created ragdoll cats by selectively breeding the kittens of a cat named Josephine. Her kittens were particularly sweet. These beautiful cats had a special quality. They tended to go limp in one's arms when picked up. Baker called the new breed "ragdoll" for this reason.

126

APPEARANCE

Ragdoll cats have medium-long coats and large, bushy tails. They feature longer fur around their necks and on their hindquarters.

Ragdolls are a pointed breed. This means they have dark markings on their faces, ears, legs, and tails. These points can be seal, blue, chocolate, or lilac. Large, oval blue eyes contrast these markings.

Mature male ragdolls usually weigh between 15 and 20 pounds (7 and 9 kg). Females weigh around 10 to 15 pounds (4.5 to 7 kg).

BEHAVIOR

The ragdoll's sweet, friendly temperament is a big reason this breed is so popular. Ragdolls enjoy being with people and are good with children. They tend to follow their humans around the house. Ragdolls also get along well with other pets, including dogs. Ragdolls are laid back but also very social. These curious, people-loving felines may even greet guests at the door.

KITTENS

Mother ragdolls can have up to three litters per year. Each litter will contain an average of four kittens. Ragdoll kittens are born nearly all white. As they get older, their fur begins to change color. The points turn the darkest because they are the coolest areas on the kitten's body.

RUSSIAN BLUE

BREED HISTORY

The Russian blue is a natural breed. It is believed that these cats began in Russia's Archangel Isles. This has led to them being called Archangel cats.

Knowledge of the Russian blue's beginnings is lost to history. However, some legends say Russian blues may have been hunted for their unusual fur. Others claim Russian blues were favorite cats of czars.

APPEARANCE

The Russian blue cat has a very dense coat. The double coat is water resistant. This breed only comes in the coat color blue. The coat's blue guard hairs are tipped in silver. The coat looks beautiful with the cat's eyes. The breed's large, round eyes come in only one color. That color is a striking green. Female Russian blues weigh between 7 and 10 pounds (3 and 4.5 kg). Males are larger at 10 to 12 pounds (4.5 to 5.4 kg).

BEHAVIOR

Russian blues are cautious cats. They take time to observe what is happening before entering a situation. Because they are shy, people think blues are not friendly. But once they decide you are worthy, blues are wonderful companions.

When Russian blues are comfortable in their homes, they are playful. Blues are also smart. They can learn how to open drawers to get to hidden things.

KITTENS

Kittens weigh just 2 to 3 ounces (57 to 85 g) at birth. After ten to 12 days, they can see and hear. Their teeth begin to grow in. When they are three weeks old, they begin to explore the world.

Russian blue cats are born with blue eyes. The color then changes to khaki or gold. By four months old, the eyes should have some green in them. The eyes will be their final green color when the kittens are one year old.

SAFARI

BREED HISTORY

A wildcat called Geoffroy's cat lives in South America. Some people keep them as pets. Others breed Geoffroy's cats with domestic cats. This creates a hybrid cat called the safari. The safari is one of the rarest designer cats.

APPEARANCE

The safari comes in three different colors. The coat can be gold with black spots. It can be black with darker black spots. Or the safari can have a silver base coat with black markings. However, that is more unusual.

Safari cats are among the largest hybrid cats. There are reports from the 1970s of males weighing 36 pounds (16 kg). Generally, adult males can reach 25 pounds (11 kg). Female safari cats are smaller than males. However, fully grown females can still tip the scales at around 18 pounds (8 kg).

BEHAVIOR

Like many hybrid cats, safaris have a lot of energy. They are usually on the move, running and climbing. Since these cats are good at climbing, it's important for owners to have a vertical space for the cats to play with.

KITTENS

Creating safari cats is difficult. Since the time this hybrid was first bred, few males have been produced. This cat is very rare.

BREED HISTORY

The savannah cat is a cross between a serval—a wildcat native to Africa—and a domestic cat. The first savannah kitten was born on April 7, 1986. Breeder Judee Frank successfully bred a male African serval with a female domestic cat. Another breeder named Suzi Wood named the kitten Savannah. Eventually, this became the name of the hybrid, too.

Savannah went on to produce numerous litters. Cat enthusiast Patrick Kelley purchased one of Savannah's kittens. He then worked with breeder Joyce Sroufe to further develop the hybrid. Sroufe became a successful savannah breeder. In 1997, she introduced the savannah cat to the public. Today, savannahs are rare. That is because breeding savannahs is difficult. Mating a serval with a domestic cat is not always successful.

APPEARANCE

The savannah's coat is short to medium in length. It lies close to the body. Coarse guard hairs cover a soft undercoat. Yet, spots on the coat have a soft feel to them. Savannah colors can be black, black smoke, brown spotted tabby, or silver spotted tabby. A spotted savannah has bold dark-brown to black spots. Stripes run from the back of the head to just over the shoulders.

The savannah also has dark tearstain markings. These markings start at the inner corner of each eye. They run down the sides of the nose to the whisker area.

Male savannahs range from 15 to 30 pounds (7 to 14 kg). Females weigh between 9 and 17 pounds (4 and 8 kg).

BEHAVIOR

Savannahs are friendly, playful, and energetic. Unlike many domestic cats, savannahs like water. Some savannahs may wait by the door for their owners to come home. These loving cats will even follow their owners around the house. These cats can be trained. Some owners report their cats can play fetch and perform simple tricks. They can even be trained to walk on a leash when outside.

Savannahs are high-energy, active cats. Owners need to have plenty of toys on hand. And they must take time to play with their cats. Some places in the United States do not allow people to own savannah cats because of the cat's wild roots.

KITTENS

Savannah kittens take three years to reach full size. The size of a savannah will depend on its generation. This refers to how closely related the savannah is to the original serval parent. The closer the savannah is to the serval, the larger it will be.

BREED HISTORY

The first Scottish fold was discovered in Coupar Angus, Scotland. In 1961, William Ross found a cat with folded ears in a litter of domestic cats. The cat was named Susie.

Later, Susie had a litter of kittens. Two of the kittens had folded ears. Ross and his wife Mary took one of the folded-ear kittens home. They named her Snooks. The Rosses bred Snooks, and the Scottish fold breed began.

Scottish fold cats are bred with American or British shorthair cats with straight ears. Usually, some kittens in a litter will have the folded-ear trait. Scottish fold cats with folded ears should never be bred together. Kittens that have two folded-ear parents often have abnormal cartilage. This can cause stiffness in joints such as the knee and tail.

APPEARANCE

Scottish folds are medium-sized cats. They can have three kinds of folded ears. Slightly folded ears are called single fold. If the ears are folded about halfway, it is called double fold. Triple-fold ears lie flat against the head. This is the most desirable ear.

Scottish fold cats can have short or long hair. The short-haired Scottish fold's coat is medium-short in length. The longhair breed has a medium-long coat. Both breeds' coats are plush, dense, and soft to the touch. They come in every color except point colors, such as Siamese colors.

BEHAVIOR

Scottish folds are friendly cats. They are quiet, gentle, reserved, and intelligent. They can easily adapt to any living situation. Scottish folds get along well with children and other pets.

They have sweet, quiet voices. But you will not hear them often.

Scottish fold cats are loving and friendly and do not demand attention. They will sit on your lap when you want them to. But they will not be bothered if you don't pay close attention to them. Scottish folds do not need to be involved in what is going on around them. They will be fine if left alone, but if an owner is going away for a long period of time, these cats will get lonely.

KITTENS

Scottish folds usually have about five kittens in a litter. All are born with straight ears. Only about half will develop folded ears.

SELKIRK REX

BREED HISTORY

In 1987, Montana cat breeder Jeri Newman received a call from a local animal shelter. Shelter workers had a kitten with an unusual curly coat. They thought she might want the kitten. Newman adopted it. The kitten was kind of bossy. So, Newman named her Pest.

Newman was interested in cat genetics. Pest's curly coat was intriguing. Newman wondered if Pest's kittens would inherit these features. So, she bred Pest with a male Persian cat.

Pest delivered a litter of six kittens. Three of them had curly hair. This meant the gene for curly hair would pass from generation to generation. Newman continued to develop the breed. This breed is called the Selkirk rex.

APPEARANCE

The breed's plush, soft coat resembles that of a woolly sheep. The undercoat is dense with fine, curly hair. The outercoat's guard hairs are soft to the touch.

The Selkirk rex can have a short coat or a long coat. Selkirks can be any color. White, black, blue, red, and cream are common coat colors. In addition to a wide variety in color, their coats have many possible patterns.

Males weigh 11 to 16 pounds (5 to 7 kg). Females are slightly lighter at 6 to 12 pounds (2.7 to 5.4 kg).

BEHAVIOR

Selkirks are loving and affectionate cats. They are tolerant of children and like to be held and cuddled. They attach themselves to one person, following that person everywhere.

These calm, quiet cats are also playful. They enjoy playing fetch and other games, especially with a favorite person. Selkirks are also intelligent and can be trained. They respond well to positive attention.

KITTENS

A mother Selkirk has about three to five kittens in a typical litter.

SIAMESE

BREED HISTORY

The Siamese cat was first discovered in Siam. Today, Siam is called Thailand. In Siam, visitors were charmed by these beautiful cats. Soon, the cats were brought to other countries.

APPEARANCE

It is easy to recognize a Siamese cat. Its short, silky coat is uniquely colored. The fur on the cat's points is darker than the rest of the body. The points are the cat's ears, face, legs, and tail.

A Siamese cat may be one of four colors. A seal point cat has a cream-colored body. Its seal brown points look almost black. A blue point cat has a bluish-white body. Its points are slate blue. Chocolate point Siamese have ivory bodies with chocolate-brown points. Lilac point cats have white bodies. Their points are pinkish gray. Siamese can weigh between 6 to 14 pounds (3 to 6 kg).

BEHAVIOR

These cats are curious. So, they need owners who can give them lots of attention. They appreciate feline companions, too. These intelligent cats like to be around their people. They are loving and affectionate.

Siamese cats are playful and outgoing. They will not tolerate being ignored. In fact, these cats are very talkative.

KITTENS

A female Siamese cat usually gives birth to four kittens in each litter. Siamese kittens are born white. Their points gradually gain color as they get older. Siamese kittens should be handled gently every day. This will create calm, friendly pets.

SIBERIAN

BREED HISTORY

Siberian cats come from Russia. They are an ancient breed. Russians have adored them for hundreds of years. The first Siberians arrived in the United States in 1990.

APPEARANCE

Siberian cats have long, thick coats. Their coats have different layers. The top layer is coarse and waterproof. The undercoat is dense and soft. In the winter, the coat is thick and full. In the summer, Siberians shed. The thinner coat keeps them cool.

Siberians come in many colors. The most common are brown, red, black, and white. Sometimes, Siberians are one solid color. Other times, the colors combine.

Siberians also come in a variety of patterns. Calico Siberians have patches of color all over their bodies. Siberian tabbies have striped fur. Pointed Siberians have dark legs, tails, and faces.

Siberians are large cats. They take five years to reach full size. They can weigh between 12 to 20 pounds (5.4 to 9 kg).

BEHAVIOR

Siberian cats are energetic and playful. They are good with young children and other pets. Siberians are also calm, easygoing, and curious.

Siberians have another important trait. They have low levels of Fel D1. Fel D1 is an allergen that causes most cat allergies. This means Siberians sometimes make good pets for people who are allergic to other cats. They can still cause allergies in some people, however.

KITTENS

A female cat can have kittens when she is close to one year old. Then she finds a warm, quiet place to deliver her kittens. Mother Siberians have about four to six kittens in a litter.

SINGAPURA

BREED HISTORY

Singapura is the Malaysian word for Singapore. That is the country where these cats came from. In Singapore, the cats were simply known as street, sewer, or drain cats. The breed's exact origin is unknown. However, its coat color and pattern are found in cats from Southeast Asia.

APPEARANCE

The Singapura's coat color is called sepia agouti. This special color is an ivory base color with a dark-brown ticked tabby pattern. In this pattern, individual hairs have bands of light and dark color. All strands end in a dark tip.

The Singapura's chest, muzzle, and chin are lighter in color. The inside of each front leg has signature markings, or barring. These markings are also on the knee of each rear leg.

Unlike many breeds, the Singapura has only one layer of hair. There is no downy undercoat. The single layer is short and silky. It lies close to the skin, giving the breed its sleek look. Female Singapuras are small, weighing just 5 to 6 pounds (2 to 3 kg). Males are slightly larger, weighing up to 8 pounds (4 kg).

BEHAVIOR

The Singapura is a highly affectionate breed. Your Singapura will want to be with you or on you at all times. This makes the breed dearly loved by many, but too needy for others.

Singapuras love and seek constant attention. They are best suited for families that are home a lot. For busy families, having other cats can help provide interaction. Singapuras also get along well with children, but they don't like loud noises.

The Singapura is a curious, intelligent cat. It wants to be involved in human activities, whether it's invited or not.

KITTENS

Singapura cats do not reproduce until they are at least one year old. An average litter size is four kittens. The Singapura is smaller than many other cat breeds, so the kittens are very tiny.

SOMALI

BREED HISTORY

Somali cats are a fairly new breed. However, their closest relative is the Abyssinian. This is one of the oldest domestic cat breeds in the world.

Somalis are similar to Abyssinians in every way except hair length. Abyssinians are a short-haired breed. Throughout history, long-haired kittens appeared in Abyssinian litters.

In the 1960s, breeders decided to take these long-haired Abyssinian kittens and create a new breed. American breeder Evelyn Mague named the breed Somali.

APPEARANCE

The Somali is a medium-sized cat with a lean, muscular body. Somalis are actually considered a semi-longhaired cat. Their soft, silky hair is medium length. It appears longer around the neck, hindquarters, and tail. But the hair is shorter on the shoulders and body.

The Somali's fur is flecked with ticking. A ticked coat has a base color that is interrupted by two to three bands of darker color. Also, the back of the Somali's hind legs and its paw pads are always darker than the coat. Somalis can be many colors including blue, fawn, red, and ruddy.

BEHAVIOR

Somalis are smart, sociable cats that need a lot of attention. They love the outdoors and should not be confined or left alone for long periods of time. Somalis get along well with other pets, too.

Somalis show a lively interest in everything. They often open cabinets and drawers. Sometimes, they will carry objects around in their mouths. They have also been known to eat things they shouldn't.

Somalis are active and playful. They love toys and playing fetch. These cats will even invent their own games.

KITTENS

Somali kittens are born with dark coats that gradually lighten as they get older. It can take up to two years for their full coat colors to be established.

TABBY

TABBY COLOR HISTORY

Though there are more than 40 different cat breeds, tabby is not one of them. Tabby is a type of coat coloring. All cats with this coat type are called tabby cats.

The tabby coat comes from the domestic cat's African wildcat ancestors. The coat patterns provided the camouflage these cats needed to survive in the wild. Today, the tabby coat occurs in many different cat breeds.

APPEARANCE

A tabby's size depends on its breed. There are four types of tabby patterns. Each has different markings. Parallel stripes line the sides of a mackerel tabby. A classic tabby displays swirl patterns on its sides. Spots make the spotted tabby stand out. The ticked tabby does not have stripes, swirls, or spots. It has tabby markings on its face and tail. Many tabbies have a mark shaped like an *M* on their foreheads.

Tabby patterns come in many colors. A brown tabby has black markings on a brown or gray coat. A tabby with gray markings on a lighter gray or buff coat is called blue. The recognizable red tabby has orange markings on a cream coat. A cream tabby has cream markings on a pale cream coat. A silver tabby can have black, blue, cream, or red markings. A tabby cat's eye color depends on its coat color. Its eyes can be blue, gold, green, or hazel.

BEHAVIOR

A tabby cat's qualities are associated with its breed. Many tabby cats are mixed-breed cats. These working cats catch mice in homes and barns. They can make good house cats and companion animals.

Other tabby cats are purebred cats. For instance, brown tabby is the most popular Maine coon cat color. The Cornish rex has a short, wavy coat that comes in a variety of tabby colors.

KITTENS

The size of a tabby cat's litter depends on her breed. Most tabby cat litters have about four kittens.

TOYGER

BREED HISTORY

The toyger is bred to look like a small version of the Asian tiger. However, the toyger has no tiger blood. It is a cross between a domestic shorthair tabby cat and a Bengal cat. Judy Sugden bred the first toyger in the 1980s. She hoped to create a domestic cat that looked like a tiger. The toyger breed is still a work in progress. Each generation comes one step closer to matching the striking look of the tiger.

APPEARANCE

The toyger coat is short with thick, luxurious, soft fur. It must also be glittery. The ideal toyger coat is a bright pumpkin color with very dark stripes. Like a tiger, the stripes should be bold and nonuniform.

The toyger's throat, chin, and cheeks should be white. White fur should also surround the eyes and the lower whiskers. This coloring should sweep upward onto the temples and the forehead. The paw pads and the tip of the tail must be black. Toygers can weigh between 7 to 15 pounds (3 to 7 kg).

BEHAVIOR

Toygers can make great pets. Some owners compare their toygers to dogs. Toygers are dependable, affectionate, and gentle. They can even learn to walk on a leash. These cats can also be very alert and athletic. They like active play with toys and people.

Toygers are family friendly, too. Their sizes and personalities make them suitable for most households. Toygers enjoy being around people, including children. They also get along well with other pets.

KITTENS

Most newborn kittens weigh just 3.5 ounces (99 g). They cannot see or hear. All domestic kittens depend on their mothers for care.

BREED HISTORY

Historians believe the Turkish Angora originated in Ankara, Turkey. The first written record of the breed was in France in the 1500s. By the late 1800s, the breed was established in England.

APPEARANCE

The Turkish Angora's coat is medium-long, soft, and silky. Its finely textured single coat does not mat easily, and it lies close to the body. The breed's coat comes in many colors, including solid, calico, tabby, and tortoiseshell. White coats are very popular too.

Sometimes, cats with white coats and blue eyes can be deaf. Approximately half of these cats have a genetic defect that causes this condition. Turkish Angoras can weigh between 8 to 11 pounds (4 to 5 kg).

BEHAVIOR

Though thin, the Angora's body is muscular and agile. This can get it into trouble. Tightrope walking atop doors and along curtain rods allows the breed to oversee all activity below.

Turkish Angoras are active cats. This playful breed is easily entertained. Batting small objects to the floor is a favorite activity.

Turkish Angoras are lovable and adoring. They bond with their families and are also friendly to strangers. Many Angoras are eager to greet anyone who enters their domains.

KITTENS

A female Turkish Angora can have as many as eight kittens. Turkish Angoras are usually healthy. However, the breed can have health conditions. Kittens with Turkish Angora Ataxia cannot control their muscles. And a kitten of any breed with a different blood type than its mother can get very sick.

BREED HISTORY

Turkish Vans are an ancient breed. They come from the Lake Van area of Turkey. They are also found in parts of Armenia, Syria, Iran, and Iraq. Turkish Vans are one of the earliest-known domestic breeds. They have survived unchanged for thousands of years.

APPEARANCE

Turkish Vans have white coats. They have red or brown markings on their heads and tails. This type of marking is called the Van pattern. Some Turkish Vans are solid white. These cats are known as Turkish Vankedisi cats.

The Turkish Van is a semi-long-haired cat. It does not have an undercoat like most cats. It has a water-resistant coat. A Turkish Van's coat changes with the seasons. In the summer, it has a short coat. This keeps the cat cool on hot days. In the winter, it has a long coat. This keeps the cat warm in cold weather.

Adult males weigh 10 to 20 pounds (4.5 to 9 kg). Females are lighter. They can weigh 7 to 12 pounds (3 to 5.4 kg).

BEHAVIOR

Unlike most cat breeds, the Turkish Van enjoys water. Some Turkish Vans can turn on faucets with their paws. They like to play with running water.

Turkish Vans are often compared to dogs. They can fetch toys, growl, and learn tricks. Turkish Vans can also be taught to walk on a leash.

Despite their similarities to dogs, Turkish Vans like to have space. These cats do not like to be handled. They dislike being picked up or cuddled. Turkish Vans make good pets for families with older children and adults.

KITTENS

Turkish Vans are born with thin coats. Their coats thicken as the kittens grow over the next three to five years.

AMERICAN SHORTHAIR

- Behavior: Loving and mellow
- Where It Comes From: United States
- What It Looks Like: These cats are muscular and stocky. They come in many colors, such as blue, white, red, black, silver, and cream.

American shorthair

Khao manee

KHAO MANEE

- Behavior: Smart and curious
- Where It Comes From: Thailand
- What It Looks Like: These cats have a white coat and green, gold, blue, or mismatched eyes.

LaPERM

- Behavior: Loving, hyper, and gentle
- Where It Comes From: United States
- What It Looks Like: These cats have curly or wavy coats.

LaPerm

Lykoi

LYKOI

- **Behavior:** Smart and loving
- **Where It Comes From:** United States
- **What It Looks Like:** These cats are partially hairless and don't have undercoats.

MINSKIN

- **Behavior:** Outgoing and loving
- **Where It Comes From:** United States
- **What It Looks Like:** These cats stay small and have large eyes and short legs.

Minskin

Munchkin

MUNCHKIN

- **Behavior:** Friendly, loving, and smart
- **Where It Comes From:** United States
- **What It Looks Like:** These cats have short legs and thick bodies.

NEBELUNG

- **Behavior:** Shy, doesn't like noise
- **Where It Comes From:** United States
- **What It Looks Like:** These cats have long hair and their coats are blue.

Nebelung

Peterbald

PETERBALD

- **Behavior:** Smart, curious, and social
- **Where It Comes From:** Russia
- **What It Looks Like:** These cats are small and either have short coats or no hair at all.

SNOWSHOE

- **Behavior:** Social, smart, and needy
- **Where It Comes From:** United States
- **What It Looks Like:** These cats have all-white feet and blue eyes.

Snowshoe

SPHYNX

- **Behavior:** Curious and affectionate
- **Where It Comes From:** Canada
- **What It Looks Like:** These cats are often hairless and come in colors such as chocolate, lavender, cinnamon, red, blue, white, black, and cream.

Sphynx

Tonkinese

TONKINESE

- **Behavior:** Playful, active, and needy
- **Where It Comes From:** United States
- **What It Looks Like:** These cats have a silky coat that comes in many colors, such as blue, champagne, and platinum.

CAT CARE

NECESSITIES

Cats are known as independent creatures, but they depend on owners for their care. Cats will want to bury their waste. So owners need to provide a litter box and make sure to clean it out every day. A scratching post will keep a cat from sharpening its claws on furniture and carpet. Cats will also need toys to fetch and bat around.

VET CHECKUPS

Cats require regular checkups with a veterinarian. They will receive vaccines and an overall exam at their vet visits. The vet can also spay or neuter cats that will not be bred.

GROOMING

Owners should know what type of grooming is expected for their cats. Some cats shed a lot, while others don't.

RESEARCH

Many cats need attention from their owners. Some breeds are active and can be demanding. People should do lots of research before picking out a cat. It's important to pick a type of cat that will fit with the owner's lifestyle.

Many cats have
an urge to scratch
things, so a scratching
post is necessary.

GLOSSARY

allergen
A substance that causes an allergy.

breeder
A person who raises animals. Raising animals is often called breeding them.

buff
A light yellow color.

cartilage
The soft, elastic connective tissue in the skeleton. A person's nose and ears are made of cartilage.

domesticated
Adapted to live with humans.

genetics
A branch of biology that deals with heredity.

matting
Forming into a tangled mass.

parti-color
Having a dominant color broken up by patches of one or more other colors.

pointed
Having a darker color on the head, paws, and tail.

purebred
Having parents who are both from the same breed.

shed
To cast off hair, feathers, skin, or other coverings or parts by a natural process.

tabby
A coat pattern featuring stripes or splotches of a dark color on a lighter background. Individual hairs are banded with light and dark colors.

ticked
Having hair banded with two or more colors.

FURTHER READINGS

Cats: Facts at Your Fingertips. DK Publishing, 2020.

Cinotto, Laurie. *The Itty Bitty Kitty Committee*. Roaring Brook, 2014.

Drimmer, Stephanie Warren and Gary Weitzman. *Cat Breed Guide: A Complete Reference to Your Purr-fect Best Friend*. National Geographic, 2019.

ONLINE RESOURCES

To learn more about cats, please visit **abdobooklinks.com** or scan this QR code. These links are routinely monitored and updated to provide the most current information available.

INDEX

PHOTO CREDITS

Previously titled The Cat Encyclopedia for Kids

First Edition
First Paperback Printing, 2022

THIS BOOK CONTAINS
RECYCLED MATERIALS

Editor: Alyssa Sorenson
Series Designer: Colleen McLaren
Cover Designer: Karli Kruse

ISBN: 978-1-952455-00-1 (paperback)

Library of Congress Control Number: 2022901469

Distributed in paperback by North Star Editions, Inc.
2297 Waters Drive
Mendota Heights, MN 55120
www.northstareditions.com

Printed in the United States of America